Just BELIEVE

THE WIT & WISDOM OF TED LASSO

© Danann Media Publishing Limited 2024

First published in the UK by Sona Books, an imprint of Danann Media Publishing Limited

WARNING: For private domestic use only, any unauthorised copying, hiring, lending or public performance of this book is illegal.

CAT NO. SONO603

Compiled by Iain Spragg
Cover design: Darren Grice
Book design: Darren Grice & Luke Griffin
Editor: Martin Corteel
Proof reader: Juliette O'Neill

All rights reserved. No part of this title may be reproduced or transmitted in any material form (including photocopying or storing it in any medium by electronic means and whether or not transiently or incidentally to some other use of this publication) without the written permission of the copyright owner, except in accordance with the provisions of the Copyright, Designs and Patents Act 1988. Applications for the copyright owner's written permission should be addressed to the publisher.

This is an independent publication and it is unofficial and unauthorised and as such has no connection with the Ted Lasso TV series or the characters featured in the TV series.

Printed in UAE

ISBN: 978-1-915343-61-1

THE WIT & WISDOM OF
TED LASSO

Fully Independent and Unofficial

CONTENTS

INTRODUCTION	6
THE CAST	10
THE TED LASSO FAMILY	12
MAIN CHARACTERS	23
RECURRING CHARACTERS	24
GUEST APPEARANCES	26
CAMEOS	28
CELEBRITY FANS	30
TED LASSO'S BEST QUOTES	32
THE LASSO FAMILY'S BEST QUOTES	90
THE 'REAL-LIFE' TEDS	124
TED LASSO TRIVIA	144

INTRODUCTION

An award-winning TV hit with a worldwide army of fans, **TED LASSO** burst onto our screens in 2020 and over three poignant seasons has made viewers laugh and cry in equal measure. Although the show is centred around football and the fluctuating fortunes of the fictional **AFC RICHMOND**, it is as much about the characters connected to the club as it is the beautiful game and their trials and tribulations both on and off the pitch.

INTRODUCTION

The eponymous **TED LASSO**, who hails from **KANSAS**, is like a man like many **AMERICANS** who believes **'FOOTBALL'** is played with helmets, shoulder pads and an oval rather than round ball. When he is unexpectedly hired by **RICHMOND** to be the club's new manager, he predictably struggles to come to terms with life in the **UK** and is as confused by the laws and traditions of the game as he is by the **BRITISH** love affair with tea.

He's oblivious that his job is part of the owner's secret plan to ruin **RICHMOND** and in his first season in charge, the club are dramatically relegated. **TED'S** 'bouncebackability' isn't in short supply however and he triumphantly leads the team back to the **PREMIER LEAGUE** at the first time of asking. In his third and final season in the dugout, **RICHMOND** are almost crowned champions.

The show revolves around **TED**, charming, kind and almost always unflappable, but he's kept hilarious company by a long list of characters who are beyond sceptical when he arrives at the club but come to love and respect him. The **'LASSO FAMILY'** keeps growing and although there are many both funny and sad dramas on their journey, its members all benefit from a bit of **TED** time.

INTRODUCTION

TED LASSO was a massive success from the start. Viewers loved it and the First Season of the show was nominated for 20 **EMMY AWARDS** in 2020, a record for a new comedy. In total it has received 61 **EMMY** nominations over its three series but more importantly became a show which put **'SOCCER'** on the primetime map.

TED LASSO

THE CAST

TED LASSO THE CAST

THE TED LASSO FAMILY

TED LASSO
(JASON SUDEIKIS)

An amiable **AMERICAN** who crosses the Atlantic in a bizarre move to become the manager of **AFC RICHMOND** in the **PREMIER LEAGUE**. **TED** knows nothing about the beautiful game, least of all the offside rule, having only coached **AMERICAN FOOTBALL** at college level back home. At first mocked by the club's fans, his own players and the media as a fish out of water, **TED** wins them over with his natural compassion, humour, unshakeable optimism and, eventually, some victories on the pitch. Throughout the series he experiences divorce and crippling anxiety, as well as trying to come to terms with his father's suicide, but unfailingly makes friends along the way.

TED LASSO

JUST BELIEVE - THE WIT & WISDOM OF TED LASSO

REBECCA WELTON
(HANNAH WADDINGHAM)

REBECCA WELTON

The new boss of **AFC RICHMOND**, **REBECCA** hires **TED** with the intention of him overseeing a disastrous season because of his ineptitude, an act of revenge following her acrimonious divorce from her ex-husband **RUPERT**, who previously owned the club. **REBECCA'S** frosty, ruthless exterior begins to **MELT** as the show unfolds and she and **TED** become friends after she confesses her secret motive behind his new job and later helps him when he suffers from panic attacks. They also bond over his daily delivery of **HOMEMADE BISCUITS** to her office.

ROY KENT
(BRETT GOLDSTEIN)

The ageing and always angry captain of **AFC RICHMOND** at the beginning of **TED LASSO**, the character is based on **MAN UNITED** hardman **ROY KEANE**. Club legend **ROY KENT** retires at the end of Season One, but after a foul-mouthed stint as a TV pundit he rejoins **RICHMOND** as a coach, and at the end of Season Three replaces the departing **TED** as manager. Emotionally repressed at first, he slowly mellows after he hangs up his boots. He has an on-off romance with the club's head of PR **KEELEY JONES** and ongoing hate and finally love relationship with egotistical star striker **JAMIE TARTT**.

ROY KENT

KEELEY JONES
(JUNO TEMPLE)

Professionally admired and romantically desired by many of the other characters in the show, **KEELEY** is a former glamour model and social media influencer turned PR guru. In her own words she is "sort of famous for almost being famous" but unlike many of her peers, proves she has a natural knack for the media business as well as good looks. **KEELEY'S** love life is nothing if not complicated but seeks solace and advice from **REBECCA**, who takes her under her wing after offering her a job at the club.

KEELEY JONES

TED LASSO THE CAST

JAMIE TARTT
(PHIL DUNSTER)

On loan at **RICHMOND** from **MANCHESTER CITY**, **JAMIE** is brash, insensitive and arrogant but undeniably talented. He leaves the club at the end of Season One but after appearing on a **LOVE ISLAND** style reality TV show, he returns to **LONDON** and eventually makes his peace with **TED** and his former team-mates, as well as his overbearing, alcoholic father. **KEELEY'S** first boyfriend in the show, **JAMIE** is first lost but finally found as he transforms from a selfish, self-centred character into a more mature and kind person.

JAMIE TARTT

NATE SHELLEY
(NICK MOHAMMED)

NATE SHELLEY

Unlucky and painfully unconfident in love, **NATE** is a shy and unassuming character who starts the show as the club's kitman but has an untapped talent for tactics and eventually gets promoted to the coaching staff. He later betrays **RICHMOND** and **TED** when he takes the job as **WEST HAM UNITED** manager but later quits. He is eventually forgiven for his disloyalty and returns to the club as assistant kit man under his replacement **WILL**, completing his redemption. **NATE** is another character with 'father issues' who finally finds the woman of his dreams.

COACH BEARD
(BRENDAN HUNT)

TED'S right-hand man and long-standing friend from their college days in the States, **COACH BEARD** is an enigmatic and well-read man with a criminal past but someone who actually knows something about football and how it's played.

After arriving in the **UK** he begins a fiery relationship with **JANE** and at the climax of the show, as he and **TED** sit on a plane ready to fly home to **AMERICA**, he decides to stay and marry her. Simply called **COACH BEARD** for the first 33 of **TED LASSO'S** 34 episodes, it is finally revealed that his first name is **WILLIS**.

COACH BEARD

LESLIE HIGGINS
(JEREMY SWIFT)

A jazz-loving, double bass playing family man with five sons, **HIGGINS** is at first a bullied 'yes' man at **RICHMOND** but grows into a respected elder statesman with kind and wise words for anyone who wants to listen. He's promoted to the club's **DIRECTOR OF FOOTBALL OPERATIONS**, a bribe in return for helping **REBECCA** and her plan to sabotage the team. He quits when he can no longer go along with the deceit but she successfully begs him to come back. **HIGGINS** has been happily married for 30 years, insisting his "relationship is the oxygen that gives me life."

LESLIE HIGGINS

TED LASSO THE CAST

TRENT CRIMM
(JAMES LANCE)

A hardened football reporter for ***THE INDEPENDENT***, **TRENT** is initially sceptical about **TED'S** shock appointment but changes his mind after spending time with **RICHMOND'S** new manager. He loses his job at the newspaper when he reveals it was **NATE** who had tipped him off for an exclusive about **TED'S** secret panic attacks. He returns in Season Three to write a book about the club which he initially calls ***THE LASSO WAY***, but at **TED'S** modest request changes the title to ***THE RICHMOND WAY***.

TRENT CRIMM

FULL CAST LIST

TED LASSO THE CAST

MAIN CHARACTERS

SARAH NILES as **DR SHARON FIELDSTONE**. Sport psychologist

ANTHONY HEAD as **RUPERT MANNION**. Rebecca's ex-husband and former owner of AFC Richmond

TOHEEB JIMOH as **SAM OBISANYA**. Richmond player

CRISTO FERNÁNDEZ as **DANI ROJAS**. Richmond player

BILLY HARRIS as **COLIN HUGHES**. Richmond player

JUST BELIEVE – THE WIT & WISDOM OF TED LASSO

RECURRING CHARACTERS

STEPHEN MANAS as **RICHARD MONTLAUR**. Richmond player

MOE JEUDY-LAMOUR as **THIERRY ZOREAUX**. Richmond goalkeeper

CHARLIE HISCOCK as **WILL**. Club kitman

MOHAMMED HASHIM as **MOE BUMBERCATCH**. Richmond player

ASH BAYLISS as **ARLO DIXON**. Richmond player

MAXIMILIAN OSINSKI as **ZAVA**. Richmond player

ANNETTE BADLAND as **MAE GREEN**. Local pub landlady

GUS TURNER as **HENRY LASSO**. Ted's son

ADAM COLBORNE, BRONSON WEBB and **KEVIN GARRY** as **BAZ, JEREMY** and **PAUL**. Richmond fans

KEELEY HAZELL as **BEX**. Rupert's third wife

ELLIE TAYLOR as **FLO 'SASSY' COLLINS**.

Rebecca's best friend

TOM COTCHER as **MR MANN**. OAP Richmond fan

PHOEBE WALSH as **JANE PAYNE**. Coach Beard's girlfriend

ELODIE BLOMFIELD as **PHOEBE**. Roy's niece

BILL FELLOWS as **GEORGE CARTRICK**. Former Richmond manager

RUTH BRADLEY as **MS BOWEN**. Phoebe's teacher

ANDREA ANDERS as **MICHELLE LASSO**. Ted's ex-wife

EDYTA BUDNIK as **JADE**. Nate's girlfriend

KATY WIX as **BARBARA**. Businesswoman

AMBREEN RAZIA as **SHANDY FINE**. Keeley's model friend

JODI BALFOUR as **JACK DANVERS**. Keely's girlfriend

JUST BELIEVE - THE WIT & WISDOM OF TED LASSO

GUEST APPEARANCES

KIERAN O'BRIEN as **JAMES TARTT**. Jamie's father

JIMMY AKINGBOLA as **OLLIE**. Chauffeur and waiter

KIKI MAY as **NORA**. Sassy's daughter

HARRIET WALTER as **DEBORAH**. Rebecca's mother

SAM RICHARDSON as **EDWIN AKUFO**. African billionaire

KAREN JOHAL as **NICOLE SHELLEY**. Nate's sister

SAM LIU as **MICHAEL**. Colin's boyfriend

NONSO ANOZIE as **OLA OBISANYA**. Sam's father

BECKY ANN BAKER as **DOTTIE LASSO**. Ted's mother

LEANNE BEST as **GEORGIE**. Jamie's mother

STEVE EDGE as **SIMON**. Jamie's stepfather

LLOYD GRIFFITH as **LLOYD**. Football reporter

TED LASSO THE CAST

PATRICK BALADI as **JOHN WINGSNIGHT**. Rebecca's romantic interest

PRECIOUS MUSTAPHA as **SIMI**. Chef at Sam's restaurant

ROSIE LOU as **MISS KAKES**. Rupert's West Ham assistant

MARK KEMPNER as **KENNETH.** Richmond team bus driver

SOFIA BARCLAY as **DR. O'SULLIVAN**. Roy's sister

SHAUN PRENDERGAST as a **PAPARAZZI.**

RYAN STILES and **COLIN MOCHRIE** as **LANNY** and **BRUCE**. Canadian sports commentators (voices)

EDWIN DE LA RENTA as **FRANCIS**. Edwin's assistant

SPENCER JONES as **DEREK**. Owner of Nate's favourite restaurant

SHANNON HAYES as **SHANNON**. 'Soccer Girl'

CAMEOS

The Ted Lasso team was able to persuade a host of famous football faces to appear in its three seasons, lending the show that all-important credibility. Former players **Lee Hendrie**, **Jermaine Pennant**, **George Elokobi** and **Jay Bothroyd** all featured as opposition players in Richmond games while the likes of **Eniola Aluko**, **Peter Crouch** and **Chris Powell** also accepted the invitation to join the Lasso family.

Footballers-turned-pundits and presenters also joined the party in various episodes, including big names such as **Ian Wright**, **Gary Lineker**, **Thierry Henry**, **Chris Kamara**, **Paul Merson**, **Clinton Morrison** and **Jermaine Jenas**. *Soccer Saturday* legend **Jeff Stelling** also joined the cast, as did 'real-life' referee **Mike Dean**.

TED LASSO THE CAST

The biggest cameo coup for the show came in the penultimate episode of the final season, entitled 'Mom City', when Manchester City manager **PEP GUARDIOLA** appeared as himself.

PEP GUARDIOLA

CELEBRITY FANS

According to **JASON SUDEIKIS'S**, Hollywood heart-throb **BRAD PITT** is a big fan of the show while **FRANK OZ**, the creator of *THE MUPPETS*, is another admirer. US rockers **PEARL JAM**, actor **DREW BARRYMORE**, legendary singer **DOLLY PARTON** and TV presenter **RYAN SEACREST** are avid viewers while actors and **WREXHAM** owners **RYAN REYNOLDS** and **ROB MCELHENNEY** both love **SUDEIKIS'S** work and became involved in a spoof legal argument on X after **LESLIE HIGGINS** questioned their commitment to the Welsh club.

In the UK, former *THIS MORNING* presenters **HOLLY WILLOUGHBY** and **PHILLIP SCHOFIELD** made cameos on the show as themselves, as did singer-songwriter **FLEUR EAST**. Pop icon **RICK ASTLEY** is another well-known watcher while, bizarrely, kids TV favourites the *TELETUBBIES* have given *TED LASSO* a shout-out on social media.

Perhaps the biggest fan of the show however is pop and screen queen **Jennifer Lopez**. "I know I'm a little late to the party but I feel it's one my missions in life to let everyone know about **Ted Lasso**," **JLO** wrote. "Every time I meet someone new, I just say 'have you seen **Ted Lasso**? If you guys haven't seen it, you should give it a chance. You can thank me later.'"

TED LASSO'S

BEST QUOTES

TED LASSO'S BEST QUOTES

❝❞

Coach, I got a feeling we're not in Kansas anymore.

THE SIZE OF THE CULTURAL DIVIDE BETWEEN THE US AND UK BEGINS TO DAWN ON TED

Season 1, Episode 1: 'The Pilot'

TED LASSO'S BEST QUOTES

" "

You could fill two internets with what I don't know about football.

TED OPTS FOR THE HONEST APPROACH DURING HIS FIRST PRESS CONFERENCE AS RICHMOND MANAGER

Season 1, Episode 1; 'The Pilot'

JUST BELIEVE - THE WIT & WISDOM OF TED LASSO

❝❞

You got Ronaldo and the fellow who bends it like himself.

TED SHARES HIS UNRIVALLED KNOWLEDGE OF FAMOUS FOOTBALLERS WITH THE MEDIA

Season 1, Episode 1; 'The Pilot'

TED LASSO'S BEST QUOTES

❝❞

I do. But more importantly, I think they need to believe in themselves. You know?

AFTER REBECCA TELLS HIM THE RICHMOND GROUND IS HAUNTED, TED ADMITS HE BELIEVES IN GHOSTS

Season 1, Episode 1: 'The Pilot'

> ❝❞
>
> Taking on a challenge is a lot like riding a horse, isn't it? If you're comfortable while you're doing it, you're probably doing it wrong.

TED IS READY TO GET IN THE SADDLE

Season 1, Episode 1; 'The Pilot'

TED LASSO'S BEST QUOTES

66 99

If that's a joke, I love it. If not, can't wait to unpack that with you later.

TED STRUGGLES TO COME TO TERMS WITH REBECCA'S SENSE OF HUMOUR

Season 1, Episode 1; 'The Pilot'

" "

I do love a locker room. It smells like potential.

TED IS TAKEN BY HIS NEW PLAYERS' AROMA

Season 1, Episode 1: 'The Pilot'

" "

Look, we are not playing for a tie. Ain't nobody here gonna kiss their sister. Which is an American phrase that I'm now realising does not exist here. And that's good, cause it's creepy and I hate it myself. I don't know why I said it.

Ted confirms the UK and US are two countries separated by a common language

Season 1, Episode 2: 'Biscuits'

> ❝❞
>
> If the internet has taught us anything, it's that sometimes it's easier to speak our minds anonymously.

TED IS UP TO SPEED WITH ONLINE TROLLING CULTURE

Season 1, Episode 2; 'Biscuits'

TED LASSO'S BEST QUOTES

66 99

You know what the happiest animal on earth is? It's a goldfish. You know why? Got a ten-second memory.

TED CHANNELS HIS INNER ATTENBOROUGH

Season 1, Episode 2: 'Biscuits'

JUST BELIEVE - THE WIT & WISDOM OF TED LASSO

" "

I'm gonna put it the same way the US Supreme Court did back in 1964 when they defined pornography. It ain't easy to explain but you know it when you see it.

TED ANSWERS TRENT CRIMM'S QUESTION ABOUT WHETHER HE CAN EXPLAIN THE OFFSIDE RULE

Season 1, Episode 2; 'Biscuits'

TED LASSO'S BEST QUOTES

" "

I think that you might be so sure that you're one in a million, that sometimes you forget that out there, you're just one of eleven.

TED URGES JAMIE NOT TO FORGET HIS TEAM-MATES

Season 1, Episode 2; 'Biscuits'

❝❞

What'd I tell you, huh? This woman right here is strong, confident and powerful. Boss, I tell ya, I'd hate to see you and Michelle Obama arm wrestle, but I wouldn't be able to take my eyes off it, either.

TED IS CLEARLY IMPRESSED BY REBECCA'S PHYSIQUE

Season 1, Episode 3; 'Trent Crimm: The Independent'

TED LASSO'S BEST QUOTES

" "

Love of a sports team is a lifetime obsession. Kinda like your best friend's older sister, right?

TED REVEALS A LITTLE TOO MUCH ABOUT HIS ADOLESCENT YEARS

Season 1, Episode 4; 'For The Children'

JUST BELIEVE – THE WIT & WISDOM OF TED LASSO

❝ ❞

You two knuckleheads have split our locker room in half. And when it comes to locker rooms, I like them just like my mother's bathing suits. I only wanna see them in one piece, you hear?

TED ORDERS ROY AND JAMIE TO STOP FIGHTING

Season 1, Episode 4: 'For The Children'

TED LASSO'S BEST QUOTES

" "

Fashion's all about confidence. If I didn't have any confidence, I never would've worn pyjamas to my prom and ended up in jail the rest of that night.

TED REMEMBERS HIS UNFORTUNATE BRUSH WITH THE LAW

Season 1, Episode 4: 'For The Children'

JUST BELIEVE - THE WIT & WISDOM OF TED LASSO

> ❝❞
>
> I gotta say man, sometimes you remind me of my grandma with the channel hopper. You just push all the wrong buttons.

TED REMEMBERS FAMILY FIGHTS FOR THE REMOTE CONTROL

Season 1, Episode 5; 'Tan Lines'

TED LASSO'S BEST QUOTES

" "

One more person says something me and Beard don't understand, I'm gonna have one of my son's classic temper tantrums. It's basically him calling me a bunch of silly names, you know, like dummy head or poo-poo face or poo-poo dummy.

TED REACHES BREAKING POINT AS HE STRUGGLES TO GET TO GRIPS WITH THE BEAUTIFUL GAME

Season 1, Episode 6: 'Two Aces'

66 99

No, I'm not planning on that. No, my plan is for my plan to work.

TED REFUSES TO CONSIDER THE POSSIBILITY OF FAILURE

Season 1, Episode 6: 'Two Aces'

🙶🙷

You tore your butt, son. There's nothing to be ashamed of, OK? People tear their butts all the time in athletics. You're not alone man. Hey coach, you've torn your butt a few times, right?

TED'S KNOWLEDGE OF HAMSTRING INJURIES IS QUESTIONABLE

Season 1, Episode 7; 'Make Rebecca Great Again'

JUST BELIEVE - THE WIT & WISDOM OF TED LASSO

❝ ❞

It's just a group of people who care, Roy. Not unlike folks at a hip-hop concert whose hands are not in the air.

TED EXPLAINS TO ROY THE DRESSING ROOM'S 'DIAMOND DOGS' IS JUST A SUPPORT GROUP

Season 1, Episode 8; 'The Diamond Dogs'

TED LASSO'S BEST QUOTES

> **❝ ❞**
>
> As my doctor told me when I got addicted to Fettuccine Alfredo, that's a little rich for my blood.

TED'S LOVE AFFAIR WITH PASTA BECAME A PROBLEM

Season 1, Episode 8; 'The Diamond Dogs'

JUST BELIEVE - THE WIT & WISDOM OF TED LASSO

" "

You beating yourself up is like Woody Allen playing the clarinet. I don't wanna hear it.

TED TELLS ROY TO STOP FEELING SORRY FOR HIMSELF

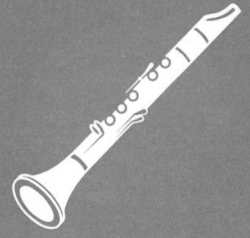

Season 1, Episode 9: 'All Apologies'

TED LASSO'S BEST QUOTES

❝❞

Your body is like day-old rice. If it ain't warmed up properly, something real bad can happen.

TED REMINDS THE SQUAD OF THE IMPORTANCE OF STRETCHING

Season 1, Episode 9; 'All Apologies'

JUST BELIEVE – THE WIT & WISDOM OF TED LASSO

" "

Ice cream's the best. It's kinda like seeing Billy Joel perform live, you know? Never disappoints. It does give me the toots though. The ice cream, not Billy Joel.

FROZEN TREATS PLAY HELL WITH TED'S DIGESTIVE SYSTEM

Season 1, Episode 9: 'All Apologies'

❝ ❞

Be honest with me. It's a prank, right? Like when us tourist folks aren't around, y'all know it tastes like garbage? You don't love it. It's pigeon sweat.

TED STRUGGLES TO COME TO TERMS WITH THE BRITISH OBSESSION WITH TEA

Season 1, Episode 9: 'All Apologies'

" "

There's two buttons I never like to hit. That's panic and snooze.

TED RESPONDS TO RICHMOND'S EARLY SEASON, SEVEN-MATCH WINLESS RUN

Season 2, Episode 1: 'Goodbye Earl'

TED LASSO'S BEST QUOTES

❝❞

I shouldn't bring an umbrella to a brainstorm.

TED REALISES HE NEEDS TO BE OPEN TO NEW IDEAS

Season 2, Episode 1; 'Goodbye Earl'

> I've never met anyone who doesn't eat sugar. Only heard about them and they all live in this godless place called Santa Monica.

TED IS SHOCKED BY DR SHARON'S DIETARY CHOICES

Season 2, Episode 2; 'Lavender'

TED LASSO'S BEST QUOTES

66 99

"I believe that Jamie's on a path to becoming a better man and I'm just here to help him along that journey. You know, think of me as his own personal Mr Miyagi. Except without all that extra yard work."

TED IS A BIG FAN OF 1980S MOVIE CLASSIC THE KARATE KID

Season 2, Episode 3; 'Do The Right-est Thing'

JUST BELIEVE - THE WIT & WISDOM OF TED LASSO

❝❞

Doing the right thing is never the wrong thing.

TED BACKS SAM AFTER HE SPARKS A PLAYER BOYCOTT OF THE CLUB'S CONTROVERSIAL SHIRT SPONSOR

Season 2, Episode 3: 'Do The Right-est Thing'

TED LASSO'S BEST QUOTES

❝ ❞

I've never been embarrassed about having streaks in my drawers. You know, it's all part of growing up.

TED MAKES LIGHT OF THE TEAM'S LOSING RUN

Season 2, Episode 3; 'Do The Right-est Thing'

❝❞

It's kinda like all the nipples in that movie Showgirls. Halfway through you don't even notice. You just kinda get sucked into the narrative.

TED REFLECTS ON YET ANOTHER EXPLETIVE-LADEN RANT FROM ROY

Season 2, Episode 5; 'Rainbow'

❝❞

Fairy tales do not start, nor do they end, in the dark forest. The son of a gun always pops up smack dab in the middle of the story. But it will all work out. Now it may not work out how you think it will or how you hope it does, but believe me it will work out.

THERE'S A POSITIVE MESSAGE SOMEWHERE IN TED'S PEP TALK

Season 2, Episode 5; 'Rainbow'

JUST BELIEVE - THE WIT & WISDOM OF TED LASSO

❝❞

People saying there's something wrong with us. Not the way I see it, OK? And here's why. I believe in Communism. Rom-Communism that is. If Tom Hanks and Meg Ryan can go through some heartfelt struggles and still end up happy, then so can we.

TED CHANNELS HOLLYWOOD TO FIRE UP THE PLAYERS

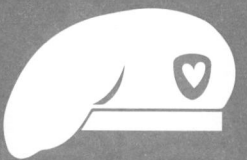

Season 2, Episode 5; 'Rainbow'

TED LASSO'S BEST QUOTES

❝ ❞

You're more mysterious than David Blaine reading a Sue Grafton novel at Area 51.

TED CAN'T GET TO GRIPS WITH DR SHARON

Season 2, Episode 6: 'The Signal'

❝❞

Boy, I love meeting people's moms. It's like reading an instruction manual as to why they're nuts.

REBECCA'S MUM MAKES QUITE AN IMPRESSION ON TED

Season 2, Episode 6; 'The Signal'

TED LASSO'S BEST QUOTES

❝❞

Living in the moment, it's a gift. That's why they call it the present.

TED IS CONVINCED EVERY DAY IS WORTH CELEBRATING

Season 2, Episode 7; 'Headspace'

" "

I watched a lot of Grey's Anatomy in my early 30s. And actually, you know, I coached football. The American kind, you know? The one with all the concussions and hullabaloo about kneeling and such.

TED EXPLAINS TO THE DOCTOR WHY HE KNOWS SO MUCH ABOUT BRAIN INJURIES

Season 2, Episode 8; 'Man City'

TED LASSO'S BEST QUOTES

❝❞

Trickle-down economics may stink, but trickle-down support smells like pizza, roses and, I assume, Viola Davis.

TED HAS A NOSE FOR DRESSING ROOM HARMONY

Season 2, Episode 11; 'Midnight Train To Royston'

❝❞

Just listen to your gut and on the way down to your gut, check in with your heart. Between those two things, they'll let you know what's what.

TED ADVOCATES A BIOLOGICAL APPROACH TO DECISION MAKING

Season 2, Episode 11; 'Midnight Train To Royston'

TED LASSO'S BEST QUOTES

❝❞

Well, you say impossible, but all I hear is 'I'm possible'.

OPTIMISM IS PART OF TED'S DNA

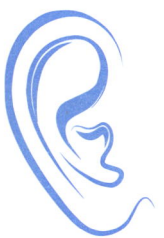

Season 2, Episode 11; 'Midnight Train To Royston'

JUST BELIEVE - THE WIT & WISDOM OF TED LASSO

> You know my philosophy with cats, babies and apologies. You gotta let them come to you.

TED EXPLAINS TO COACH BEARD THAT PATIENCE IS A VIRTUE

Season 2, Episode 12; 'Inverting The Pyramid Of Success'

TED LASSO'S BEST QUOTES

66 99

Henry and I played a whole bunch of FIFA while he was here. Very helpful. You know, we both learned who Maradona was, and I had to explain to my son why cocaine is actually bad for you.

TED LEARNS ROLE MODELS CAN BE BOTH GOOD AND BAD

Season 3, Episode 1: 'Smells Like Mean Spirit'

❝❞

You watch from now on. I'll be floating like a butterfly and stinging like a bee. Except I won't die immediately after using my stinger. I plan to float and sting for the entirety of the whole season.

TED RESPONDS TO REBECCA'S PLEA TO SHOW MORE FIGHT

Season 3, Episode 1; 'Smells Like Mean Spirit'

TED LASSO'S BEST QUOTES

66 99

I predict all their predictions ain't gonna come true. So it looks like we got ourselves a prediction Mexican standoff. Or as they call them in Mexico, a prediction standoff.

TED DOESN'T CARE THAT THE PUNDITS ARE WRITING RICHMOND OFF

Season 3, Episode 1; 'Smells Like Mean Spirit'

> "Rugby, what a game. It's like American football and sumo wrestling gave birth to a baby with huge muscular thighs all caked in mud."

TED'S DESCRIPTION OF RUGBY IS HARD TO ARGUE WITH

Season 3, Episode 1; 'Smells Like Mean Spirit'

💬

> We get one goal, we're right back in this thing, yeah? But right now, we are being so unoffensive, we might as well be a Hallmark Christmas movie, you know what I'm saying?

TED WANTS MORE AGGRESSION FROM THE TEAM

Season 3, Episode 2:
'(I Don't Want To Go To) Chelsea'

> Coaching a superstar can't be all. How do you solve a problem like Maria? Although if you ask me, the Nazis were the real problem in that story. Am I right, Coach?

TED REFLECTS ON THE CHALLENGE OF MANAGING ZAVA

Season 3, Episode 3; '4-5-1'

TED LASSO'S BEST QUOTES

" "

Don't sell yourself short. If anything, sell yourself tall and get it altered later.

TED IS AN ADVOCATE OF SELF-CONFIDENCE

Season 3, Episode 3; '4-5-1'

JUST BELIEVE - THE WIT & WISDOM OF TED LASSO

❝❞

It's not like we can handcuff him to his locker and make him love us.

TED HAS TO ACCEPT THAT ZAVA IS LEAVING THE CLUB

Season 3, Episode 5; 'Signs'

❝ ❞

All right my merry pranksters. If we're gonna play Total Football, there are four things we need to focus on. Number one, conditioning. Y'all gotta get into even better shape. Number two, versatility. Number three, awareness. And number four... I don't know what that one is yet but I know it's important.

TED'S TACTICAL PLAN IS ALMOST PERFECT

Season 3, Episode 7: 'The Strings That Bind Us'

JUST BELIEVE - THE WIT & WISDOM OF TED LASSO

❝❞

It is nearly impossible to not be fully aware of what your teammate's doing when y'all got a rope tied around your dingdong. Am I right about that Roy?

TED DEFENDS A BIZARRE TRAINING SESSION

Season 3, Episode 7; 'The Strings That Bind Us'

TED LASSO'S BEST QUOTES

66 99

The truth is, only way I could be happier is if my arm-feet were covered in barbecue sauce.

TED REACTS AFTER RICHMOND WIN EIGHT ON THE BOUNCE

Season 3, Episode 9; 'La Locker Room Aux Folles'

JUST BELIEVE - THE WIT & WISDOM OF TED LASSO

❝❞

Well fellas, if you're looking for a pep talk from me, you're in trouble. Cause I'm like Michael Flatley at 11.59pm on St. Patrick's Day, I'm tapped out.

TED IS RUNNING ON EMPTY IN THE SEASON THREE FINALE

Season 3, Episode 12; 'So Long, Farewell'

TED LASSO'S BEST QUOTES

　❝❞

Look I know folks are divided on the actual police these days, but all human beings are opposed to the laugh police.

TED DEFENDS JEREMY'S UNUSUAL LAUGH

Season 3, Episode 12; 'So Long, Farewell'

THE LASSO FAMILY'S BEST QUOTES

THE LASSO FAMILY'S BEST QUOTES

" "

Yes, he's in over his head. He insisted twice that he didn't care if Richmond won or lost. But if the Lasso's way is wrong, it's hard to imagine being right.

TRENT REVEALS HIMSELF AS TED'S UNLIKELY CHEERLEADER

Season 1, Episode 3; 'Trent Crimm: The Independent'

THE LASSO FAMILY'S BEST QUOTES

" "

"I do yoga with a group of women in their 60s. They have no idea who I am. It's twice a week and it's really good for my core. Normally only takes an hour but Maureen's been going through a divorce and she needed to talk about it and blow off some steam. We all ended up at G-A-Y until 2am and then we had crepes in Balham with some drag queens. Like I said, it's private."

ROY IS FULL OF SURPRISES

Season 1, Episode 8; 'The Diamond Dogs'

JUST BELIEVE - THE WIT & WISDOM OF TED LASSO

> Does my face look like it's in the mood for shape-based jokes?

ROY IS UNIMPRESSED WITH TED'S ADVICE ON HIS LOVE-TRIANGLE DILEMMA

Season 1, Episode 8; 'The Diamond Dogs'

THE LASSO FAMILY'S BEST QUOTES

❝ ❞

Right, I'm not going to beat around the bush. I'm just going to get straight to the point. No faffing around because that's just annoying. And definitely no procrastinating. That's a good word, isn't it? Procrastinating. I wonder what the etymology of that word is? I have no idea. Hey, why don't we look it up?

REBECCA FAILS TO PRACTICE WHAT SHE PREACHES

Season 1, Episode 9; 'All Apologies'

❝❞

"When the vinegar was next to the Heineken, they weren't offside. It's not when the vinegar catches the ball, it's when ketchup passes the ball."

COACH BEARD ATTEMPTS YET AGAIN TO EXPLAIN THE OFFSIDE RULE TO TED

Season 1, Episode 10: 'The Hope That Kills You'

THE LASSO FAMILY'S BEST QUOTES

" "

Old people are so wise.
They're like tall Yodas.

JAMIE REFLECTS ON THE WISDOM OF OAPS

Season 2, Episode 2; 'Lavender'

> ❝ ❞
>
> Jamie Carragher sent me flowers. We despised each other when we played, now he's sending me flowers. How does he know I love white orchids?

ROY WORRIES HE HAS A FAMOUS STALKER

Season 2, Episode 2; 'Lavender'

THE LASSO FAMILY'S BEST QUOTES

"

Most adults think kids need to be constantly entertained. I didn't need a parade every day growing up, did you? Truth is they just want to feel part of our lives. Little idiots!

ROY EXPLAINS HIS PARENTING PHILOSOPHY

Season 2, Episode 3;
'Do The Right-est Thing'

JUST BELIEVE - THE WIT & WISDOM OF TED LASSO

" "

Problems, they're like mushrooms. The longer you leave them in the dark, the bigger they get.

KEELEY SHINES A LIGHT ON KEEPING SECRETS

Season 2, Episode 4: 'Carol Of The Bells'

THE LASSO FAMILY'S BEST QUOTES

❝❞

To the family we're born with and to the one we make along the way.

HIGGINS MAKES THE PLAYERS FEEL AT HOME AT CHRISTMAS

Season 2, Episode 4; 'Carol Of The Bells'

JUST BELIEVE - THE WIT & WISDOM OF TED LASSO

> You buy a man a table, he eats once. You teach a man how to get a table and he eats at that restaurant until it becomes a Starbucks.

KEELEY'S KNOWLEDGE OF HOSPITALITY IS UNRIVALLED

Season 2, Episode 5; 'Rainbow'

THE LASSO FAMILY'S BEST QUOTES

> 66 99

I try to be outwardly supportive of all relationships due to my dad sabotaging one of my first loves. In Year Four he sat me and my classmate, Nadia Shookums, down in the living room and said he thought we could both do better. Well, she listened to him.

NATE'S SEARCH FOR LOVE WAS ALWAYS A STRUGGLE

Season 2, Episode 6: 'The Signal'

"

The truth will set you free.
But first it will piss you off.

DR SHARON TELLS TED THINGS WILL GET WORSE BEFORE THEY GET BETTER

Season 2, Episode 7; 'Headspace'

THE LASSO FAMILY'S BEST QUOTES

❝❞

Jamie and Dani are like Picasso and Gauguin. Artists, they're artists. And, Colin, you paint too but your work doesn't end up in museums. You're like a painting at a Holiday Inn. You don't inspire. You don't move people. You're there. You cover a bloodstain. You do the job, so just do the job.

NATE DELIVERS A HARSH LESSON

Season 2, Episode 7: 'Headspace'

> ❝ ❞
>
> I like to imagine a heaven where animals are in charge and humans are the pets. I'd like to spend eternity curled up in front of a fire at Cindy Clawford's feet.

HIGGINS REVEALS HIS DREAM AFTERLIFE

Season 2, Episode 10; 'No Weddings And A Funeral'

THE LASSO FAMILY'S BEST QUOTES

> There is something I should warn you of. I'm only going to get more wonderful.

SAM PREDICTS A BRIGHT FUTURE FOR HIMSELF

Season 2, Episode 10: 'No Weddings And A Funeral'

" "

Would Bill Shankly have a panic attack, eh? Would Brian Clough? Would Alex Ferguson have a panic attack? No, of course he wouldn't. Look, if your ship's being attacked, right? And you run to the bridge, you want to find a captain whose brain works, not some big girl's blouse.

FORMER RICHMOND MANAGER GEORGE CARTRICK BELIEVES IN CALMNESS

Season 2, Episode 12: 'Inverting The Pyramid Of Success'

THE LASSO FAMILY'S BEST QUOTES

> We ain't going to get relegated because we're together. And together, we got me.

JAMIE'S MODESTY IS LIMITLESS

Season 3, Episode 1; 'Smells Like Mean Spirit'

> Sending off Van Damme was a mistake. He played with passion. Passion is a word we use when we talk about love. It is also a word we use to describe a crime. Sometimes it is also a fruit.

YOU CANNOT FAULT ZAVA'S LINGUISTIC LOGIC

Season 3, Episode 4; 'Big Week'

THE LASSO FAMILY'S BEST QUOTES

66 99

Pain is like carbon monoxide. Expressing it to the person who hurt you is like opening a vent but holding it in will poison you.

COACH BEARD COULD HAVE BEEN A THERAPIST

Season 3, Episode 4; 'Big Week'

JUST BELIEVE - THE WIT & WISDOM OF TED LASSO

> For some reason, whenever I'm trying to impress someone, I end up sounding like my gran.

NATE ADMITS HE STRUGGLES WITH ROMANTIC SMALL TALK

Season 3, Episode 5; 'Signs'

THE LASSO FAMILY'S BEST QUOTES

❝❞

Best thing you can do with bullies is ignore them. Then you sneak into their house at 4am, which statistically is the hour people are least prepared to defend themselves. And once you're standing over them, as they sleep in their bed, you start to beat them. With a thick heavy rope soaked in red paint. Pummelling them over and over until they wake, confusing the paint for their own blood.

ROY EMBRACES HIS DARK SIDE AGAIN

Season 3, Episode 5; 'Signs'

> Prophets believe in something. I do not just believe. I know in my heart. In my bones, in my well-defined delts, traps, glutes that there is no opponent this team cannot conquer.

ZAVA ISN'T SHORT OF BODY CONFIDENCE

Season 3, Episode 5; 'Signs'

THE LASSO FAMILY'S BEST QUOTES

❝❞

The universe is full of things we can't explain. Fingernails. What's that about?

HIGGINS IS CONFUSED BY HIS HANDS

Season 3, Episode 5: 'Signs'

" "

A friendly is a pretend match. This is a pretend conversation. You're a pretend person with a pretend job. And I'm having a really hard time pretending to give a shit.

ROY'S RELATIONSHIP WITH THE MEDIA GOES FROM BAD TO WORSE

Season 3, Episode 6: 'Sunflowers'

THE LASSO FAMILY'S BEST QUOTES

❝❞

On your feet, maggots! Right. Today you're gonna run from end to end to end to end. But lucky for you, I'm in a good mood so you're only going to do that for the whole practice.

COACH ROY FAVOURS THE OLD SCHOOL APPROACH TO TRAINING

Season 3, Episode 7; 'The Strings That Bind Us'

> ❝❞
>
> Total Football is about letting go of your baggage and trusting your intuition. It's Jazz. It's Motown. It's Mamet. It's Pinter. It's Einstein. It's Keurig! It's Gaga. It's my mother proudly displaying her vibrator on the bedside table.

COACH BEARD SHARES TOO MUCH

Season 3, Episode 7; 'The Strings That Bind Us'

THE LASSO FAMILY'S BEST QUOTES

❝❞

You need to stop yesterday getting in the way of today.

REBECCA WANTS TED TO FOCUS ON THE FUTURE

Season 3, Episode 8; 'We'll Never Have Paris'

❝❞

I haven't seen 22 dudes have this good a time on grass since I saw the Grateful Dead jamming with the Black Crowes and Phish.

COACH BEARD HAS A COLOURFUL PAST

Season 3, Episode 9; 'La Locker Room Aux Folles'

THE LASSO FAMILY'S BEST QUOTES

" "

I do believe in second chances, Ted. That's why I'm still married and all my sons are still alive.

HIGGINS REVEALS THE SECRETS OF A HAPPY FAMILY

Season 3, Episode 11; 'Mom City'

JUST BELIEVE - THE WIT & WISDOM OF TED LASSO

> Change isn't about trying to be perfect. Perfection sucks. Perfect is boring.

COACH BEARD LIKES LIFE INTERESTING

Season 3, Episode 12; 'So Long, Farewell'

THE LASSO FAMILY'S BEST QUOTES

❝❞

Human beings are never going to be perfect, Roy. The best we can do is keep asking for help and accepting it when you can. And if you keep on doing that, you'll always be moving towards better.

HIGGINS SHARES PERFECT ADVICE WITH ROY

Season 3, Episode 12: 'So Long, Farewell'

THE 'REAL-LIFE TEDS

THE 'REAL-LIFE' TEDS

❝ ❞

You can talk about spirit or you can live it. We took the team to a lake in Sweden where there was no electricity. We didn't eat for five days.

JÜRGEN KLOPP

❝❞

I advise my players to have sex for short periods and with the minimum of effort. And to use positions where they are under their partners.

ANTONIO CONTE

> "

In football the worst things are excuses. Excuses mean you cannot grow or move forward.

PEP GUARDIOLA

THE 'REAL-LIFE' TEDS

❝❞

Football was what brought me close to my hero [my dad]. We sometimes lose sight of what sport is about. I have come to understand this. It's not about winning or losing, it's about the connections it makes. It connects people, cities and countries. It connects parents to their children.

ANGE POSTECOGLOU

> ❝❞
>
> My job is to allow people to dream. Make the impossible seem possible.

GARETH SOUTHGATE

THE 'REAL-LIFE' TEDS

66 99

I always tell the players, the day you think there's nothing more to learn, you have to retire.

MAURICIO POCHETTINO

❝❞

I like to make a tour round the pitch before games to look at the architecture, the colours in the stadium, the sky. To feel the atmosphere growing.

UNAI EMERY

THE 'REAL-LIFE' TEDS

> ❝❞
>
> Young players are like melons. Only when you open and taste the melon are you 100% sure that the melon is good.

JOSÉ MOURINHO

JUST BELIEVE - THE WIT & WISDOM OF TED LASSO

66 99

Someone might come close to dying, and they'll enjoy life much more than everyone else. I came close to the death of my sports career, and I enjoy everything coming my way.

VINCENT KOMPANY

THE 'REAL-LIFE' TEDS

> 　　❝❞
>
> I tell you that the coaches are like cardiologists. They have to enter the player in their hearts so that the message reaches them.

MIKEL ARTETA

> ❝ ❞
>
> Success comes on foot but leaves on horseback.

ERIK TEN HAG

THE 'REAL-LIFE' TEDS

> " "
>
> Anyone can take the wheel of the ship in calm water but it's not so easy when it's not calm water. You can't just enjoy the good times; you have to be resilient in the tough times.

SEAN DYCHE

> 66 99
>
> I once cried because I had no shoes to play football with my friends. But one day I saw a man with no feet and I realised how rich I am.

ZINEDINE ZIDANE

THE 'REAL-LIFE' TEDS

66 99

I do not listen to criticism or flattery, one weakens you and the other angers you.

DIEGO SIMEONE

> 66 99

It's not just about the words you use, but the way you use them, and the message that puts over. Also your face too and the way you project your message. If you're telling the group to stay calm, be good, and you have beads of sweat dripping down your forehead, you're in trouble.

DIDIER DESCHAMPS

THE 'REAL-LIFE' TEDS

❝❞

Football is the most important of the less important things in the world.

CARLO ANCELOTTI

❝ ❞

Football without fans is sadder than dancing with your own sister.

LUIS ENRIQUE

THE 'REAL-LIFE' TEDS

66 99

I have been doing it a long time. Does it get any easier? Can you take it all a little bit more philosophically and put it more in perspective? The tragedy is no. If anything, it gets worse.

ROY HODGSON

TED LASSO

TRIVIA

TED LASSO TRIVIA

JUST BELIEVE - THE WIT & WISDOM OF TED LASSO

The character of **TED LASSO** was born in 2013 when **JASON SUDEIKIS** appeared in a five-minute clip playing the manager of **'TOTTENHAM HOTSPURS'**. The sketch was commissioned to promote **NBC SPORTS'** deal to show the Premier League in the US and proved so popular another one was broadcast in **2014**.

SUDEIKIS came up with the character after touring a comedy show during which he played football on **PLAYSTATION** before and after every performance. "The bulk of my soccer knowledge and love comes from playing **FIFA**."

TED LASSO TRIVIA

BRETT GOLDSTEIN, who plays **ROY KENT**, was first hired on the show as a scriptwriter but fell in love with the confrontational character and recorded an audition tape, which he sent to producer **BILL LAWRENCE** to land the role.

AFC RICHMOND'S fictional home stadium, **NELSON ROAD**, is in reality **CRYSTAL PALACE'S SELHURST PARK** ground. In the show, Ted's first game as the club's new manager in Season One is against **PALACE**.

JUST BELIEVE - THE WIT & WISDOM OF TED LASSO

The **SHORTBREAD BISCUITS TED** bakes for **REBECCA** are a big hit on screen but according to actress **HANNAH WADDINGHAM**, the baked treats were "absolutely horrific" in real life.

ROY'S favourite **KEBAB RESTAURANT** has a framed picture of the player on the wall. Next to it is a signed picture of American actor **GEORGE WENDT**, who played **NORM** in the classic comedy series **CHEERS**. **WENDT** is **SUDEIKIS'S** uncle.

TED LASSO TRIVIA

The Season One, Episode Seven show when the team go to a **KARAOKE BAR** to celebrate victory was written after **SUDEIKIS** heard that **LIVERPOOL** manager **JÜRGEN KLOPP** and his players had done the same thing in real life.

AFC RICHMOND'S Latin motto, as seen in the dressing room, is **'GRADARIUS FIRMUS VICTORIA'**. It roughly translates as **'SLOW AND STEADY WINS THE RACE'**.

JUST BELIEVE - THE WIT & WISDOM OF TED LASSO

? During filming for Season Two, some of the cast including **TOHEEB JIMOH (SAM OBISANYA)** and **CRISTO FERNÁNDEZ (DANI ROJAS)** went to the 2021 FA Cup final between **LEICESTER CITY** and **CHELSEA** at **WEMBLEY**. After the game, a TV reporter failed to recognise them and interviewed them thinking they were regular fans.

TED LASSO TRIVIA

Due to popular demand when Season Two was broadcast, **APPLE TV+** released an official recipe for **TED'S SHORTBREAD BISCUITS**.

Gamers were finally able to follow in **TED'S** footsteps when **EA SPORTS** made it possible to play as **AFC RICHMOND** in **FIFA 23**.

In 2023 **TED LASSO** fans were given the chance to buy their own **BUILD-A-BEAR** soft toy of the **AFC RICHMOND** boss. The teddy comes complete with **TED'S** trademark **MOUSTACHE**, **TRACKSUIT**, **AVIATOR SUNGLASSES** and **RICHMOND SUN VISOR**.

JUST BELIEVE - THE WIT & WISDOM OF TED LASSO

When the second season aired in **2021**, social media was flooded with claims that the **ROY KENT** character was really a CGI creation and not played by **BRETT GOLDSTEIN**. The actor hit back, reassuring fans that he was a "completely real, normal human man".

TED LASSO wasn't the first acting role for **HANNAH WADDINGHAM (REBECCA)** in a fictional football series after making a 2005 cameo in the final episode of Season Four in the **ITV** show **FOOTBALLERS' WIVES.**

TED LASSO TRIVIA

One of the most-loved scenes in Season One is when **TED** unexpectedly beats **REBECCA'S** vindictive ex-husband **RUPERT (ANTHONY HEAD)** at darts in the pub. The scene was originally written to revolve around a cricket match.

The exterior shots of **TED'S** local pub, **THE CROWN AND ANCHOR**, is in real life the 300-year-old **PRINCE'S HEAD** in **RICHMOND**. The interior scenes however are shot in a studio.

In the episode 'Make Rebecca Great Again' in Season One, **REBECCA** sings **'LET IT GO'** from **DISNEY** animated box office blockbuster *FROZEN*. **DISNEY** at first refused **APPLE TV+** a licence to use the song but after seeing a preview of the scene, agreed to give permission. Plan B for the showrunners was a rendition of **'I WILL SURVIVE'** by **GLORIA GAYNOR**.

TED LASSO TRIVIA

AMERICAN President **JOE BIDEN** invited the cast of **TED LASSO** to the **WHITE HOUSE** in 2023. Actor **JAMES LANCE** stayed in character as **INDEPENDENT** sports reporter **TRENT CRIMM** and asks **TED** a question in a press conference about the **2026 WORLD CUP**.

The **TED LASSO** theme tune was co-written and performed by the lead singer of British folk band **MUMFORD & SONS, MARCUS MUMFORD'**. **SUDEIKIS** and **MARCUS** met on the famous *SATURDAY NIGHT LIVE* in 2012 and the following year **SUDEIKIS** appeared in the band's video for their single **'HOPELESS WANDERER'**.

JUST BELIEVE - THE WIT & WISDOM OF TED LASSO

At the premiere of Season Two in 2021, **SUDEIKIS** wore a black T-shirt with the words **'JADON & MARCUS & BUKAYO'** on the front. The message was a supportive reference to **JADON SANCHO**, **MARCUS RASHFORD** and **BUKAYO SAKA** who had missed penalties in **ENGLAND'S** shootout defeat to **ITALY** in the **EURO 2020** final.

In the tenth episode of the first series, **TED** has a meeting with boss **REBECCA** and when he leaves her office, he jumps and bangs his head on the top of a doorframe. The incident was completely unscripted, accidental and painful.

TED LASSO TRIVIA

Sports giant **NIKE** became a sponsor of **AFC RICHMOND** for Season Three, selling official club shirts.

The character of star striker **ZAVA** (played by **MAXIMILIAN OSINSKI** in Season Three) is based on a mix of **SWEDEN'S ZLATAN IBRAHIMOVIĆ** and **FRENCH** legend **ERIC CANTONA**.

Show producer **BILL LAWRENCE** ambushed actor **ZACH BRAFF**, who he'd worked with on the hit comedy series **SCRUBS**, while he was in **LONDON** during the filming of Season One of **TED LASSO** and persuaded him to direct the show's second episode 'Biscuits'.

JUST BELIEVE - THE WIT & WISDOM OF TED LASSO

> The show's first season was the most watched programme ever to debut on **APPLE TV+**. The viewing figures for the second series were six times higher than the first.

Actors **JEREMY SWIFT** and **MARY ROSCOE** play **LESLIE HIGGINS** and his wife **JULIE**. They are married in real life.

TED LASSO TRIVIA

The show's creators – **JASON SUDEIKIS**, **BRENDAN HUNT (COACH BEARD)** and writer **JOE KELLY** – were all members of an improvisational comedy group called 'Boom Chicago'. Despite the name, the collective was actually based in **AMSTERDAM**.

Both **NICK MOHAMMED (NATE)** and **PHIL DUNSTER (JAMIE)** auditioned for the role of **LESLIE HIGGINS** but the job went to **JEREMY SWIFT**.

JUST BELIEVE - THE WIT & WISDOM OF TED LASSO

> As the man once said, 'The harder you work, the luckier you get.'

TED ENCAPSULATES HIS RECIPE FOR SUCCESS

Season 1, Episode 1; 'The Pilot'